The Only Country Was the Color of My Skin

The Only Country Was the Color of My Skin

Kathleen Hellen

Saddle Road Press

The Only Country Was the Color of My Skin
© 2018 Kathleen Hellen

All rights reserved. No part of this book may be reproduced or transmitted in any form or by any means without written permission of the author.

Saddle Road Press
Hilo, Hawai'i
saddleroadpress.com
Author photograph by Zachary Paesani
Cover image and book design by Don Mitchell

ISBN 978-0-9969074-7-7

Contents

Prologue	13

One

Trees With No Branches/ Flowers With No Name	18
Atonement	19
Mr. Is-That-So?	20
Tōjō Eats the Stones of his Defeat	21
Occupation	23
On the Lotus of Every Compassion	24
The Girl They Hired From Snow Country	26
Leaving the Emperor's Summer House	27
Bonsai	28

Two

The World As Seen Through Bottled Coke is Bigger, Mr. Moto	30
Original Child	31
Translation	32
Breakages in Japanese	33
A Rose, Twice My Size	34
Earthquake Thunder Fire Father	36
The Girl Who Loved Mothra	37
Hide the Daughters, Hide the Rice	38
Wedding of the Foxes	40
Silent Fish, Blushing Ginger	41
"Hi, in America"	42

BUTTERFLY'S DIFFICULT KATA	44
MOON IN THE WATER	45

THREE

GEISHA	48
ORIGAMI	49
FLOATING WORLD	50
TUNNEL	52
SALMON SAYS SURRENDER	54
RICE	56
TRANSLATION	57
CHOPSTICKS	58
DREAM-BOX ESSAY	59
FORTY-EIGHT POSITIONS	60
RED JAPONICA	61
SHE WHO LISTENS TO PUCCINI	62
KATANA	63
SEVEN ENEMIES	64

FOUR

AUTOBIOGRAPHIA HYSTERIA	67
TEENAGE NINJA-GEISHA	68
IRIS AND THE BLADE	69
MANZANAR	70
TO STAND IN THE SPACES OF TREES	72

FIVE

PICTURES IN BUFANO'S GARDEN	75
FUKUSHIMA	76
EPICANTHIC FOLD	77
JAPANESQUE	78
SELF-PORTRAIT	79

Furin	80
O-Furo	81
How to Wear a Kimono	82

Six

The Way of Tea	84
Epilogue	86
Festival of Season Words	88
The Japanese Have Stopped Having Babies	89
Little Zeros	90
Sayonaras	92
Notes	95
Acknowledgments	99
About the Author	101

For my parents Etsuko and Joe, who live in this, and this, for my sons David and Zachary

Caro, come ti chiamano?

Rispondi:
Oggi il mio nome è Dolore.

Però, dite al babbo,
scrivendogli,
che il giorno del suo ritorno
Gioia, Gioia mi chiamerò.

—PUCCINI, *Madama Butterfly*, Act II

Prologue

Hello Kitty

The name tags posted on the wall of Little Tokyo's
museum are another way of saying,
"We'll make an art of it,"

like Hello Kitty,
like pretty colored maps that track the diaspora
of Japanese Peruvians, Japanese Brazilians,

the black-and-white photographs of Nisei
stripped of their belonging/s,
herded to the barracks,

collages of internment
on a panel like a silk screen—
the old man asks

what might be my interest in this place,
the subject of the tour not my experience, exactly—
not me, a half-and-half,

my mother like the woman waiting at the restaurant in the plaza
where I skipped the bento box for the tempura,
a light-haired boy
sleeping soundly in her lap,
and all the Asian women there

with white men like my father.
Another way of saying
he was a soldier.

The old man with a docent's pin is proud
he once was one of two
selected from the camps
to go to prep school.

"Work hard," he says,
and everything will be all right
if we just do
what we are told.
Be a paratrooper.
An engineer.
Volunteer.

"Everyone was nice to us," he says,
the art of not

complaining,
of saying what you want
the world to be,

but I am not the kitty
on the backpack.
The pretty fiction.

I have a mouth to tell my story.

                                            Fantastical
                                            "It," mythic

                          in the way chimeras don't exist
               except in complicated theories of replacement.
Neanderthal Denisovan Homo sapiens—the DNA's long saga.
                                          A slant
                      toward yellow circumstance,
trying not to look more white, but less myself (like Shima Kito).

                Too early for the science of the numbers. The Year 27
              begins the tale about the homely duck who thinks she is
                                    unfortunate,
                     hiding in a cave (Amateratsu's?).
             A foundling frightened by the farmer's noisy children
      (the best of all the fables, as in morally offensive).

                    How far I'd have to fly to find them!
                      Little Tokyos. The Chinatowns.

     He said, "I've noticed sometimes when you're talking, you look
                                     disinterested."
Another way of saying, "Better tape or glue your eyelids open."
              Another way of saying, "You're not beautiful."

                    These hunters slaughter flocks.
                 Better to be killed by any duck.

ONE

A record of ancient matters

Trees With No Branches/Flowers With No Names

One::
A yellow finger like a bone rose out of smoke and pointed
to the sun clocks stopped the world went white
a thousand winds rushed in

Two::
Glass that didn't shatter melted bodies burned to mattered
sticks floating bloated buildings shrugged
collapsing in radiant waves

Three::
Something in his eye besides his eye turned in
he called for his wife the tattooed pattern
dangling blackened husks the sleeve of skin

Four::
Flowers grew to excess keloid cherry
blossoms falling out of iris with a head
bigger than a human's barren stem on top

Five::
Maggots hatched in wounds that wouldn't heal
the woman indistinguishable from man
as it was in the beginning, in the end

Atonement

An erasure and collage

hallowed spirits/
divine/imperishableness/

deepest regret/profound solicitude/one hundred million
people/one/

family/good and loyal/gallant/servants
of the State/devoted/enduring/extraordinary/

settlement resorting/to the Governments/of other
nations/general trends/

the best that has been done/turned against/
the Empire/hereafter/from generation

to generation/
the [unavoidable]/effect

Mr. Is-That-So?

One might have said, "...it couldn't be averted"—hundreds leaping from the cliffs. Brothers stoned by brothers. Sons who strangled mothers. One might have pardoned his reaction as the habit of that class who live in isolation, one might have pitied this grandson of Meiji, this shy, grave boy preferring tours of Disney worlds, the little mouse still ticking when they buried him.

Tōjō Eats the Stones of his Defeat

My mother's childlike hand has printed "your dad"
on the back of the photo,

corresponding to the sepia-tone
figure of my father in the foreground
looking down over wire rims,
his desk stacked with papers.

        Slightly to the right, she writes:
"The Defense Attorney Mr. Blewitt,"
and below him,

    "The Japanese Attorney Dr. Kiyose,"
    who later became prime minister.

It is 1948. My father translates generations in disgrace.
Not confession, not surrender. Tōjō stripped of medals
at the top, with earphones, behind a stand of microphones
flanked by anonymous guards.

His eyes behind the round-rim glasses pierce through tint
from shogunate to these on trial, from Tokyo's young lions to
Meiji. Me.

His smile's reserved—as if it were absurd.
Three thousand years before you
we cultivated silk,
three thousand years from now
we will return with blades turned out.

The war is never over, never lost to wounds so near the heart.
We look into the past to know defeat. Serve
shame like stones to eat
for everyone left hungry.

The war the war the war is never over.

Occupation

A million suns discharged
in one atom of defeat

When the Ancient Voice
its utterances stilted   eccentric   unrecognizable

                barely a Voice
                crackles through the static
                of the speakers

she chooses the soldier
who gives her rice. A blanket

                        The colonel with the medals
                        has a wife

                              Roses only mean he will keep her

On the Lotus of Every Compassion

Two dolphins skim the surface of the tide at Hamamatsu.
The ocean rises to her geta near the brink. A troubled mirror.

Before she is my mother, my mother dressed in virtue is
the color of the sea. How to save face?

A child, the wrong color.

Where is the clan of the bottle and leaf?
Where is the wind of belief?

The first fin rises, dives. The smaller follows, like happiness
in glimpses, retreating. A fleet of white banners....

This is the Book of Surrender.

*The story begins with Etsuko explaining
these arts had no name.*

*Shark's fin for a cough. A copper coin inside the shoe for stiffness
in the joints.
Rituals of water and the wand, of paper tied to branches of sakaki.
He told her sticks could tell a man if he would have a son or daughter.
The old ways:*

*the blackest characters a spell, an incantation.
Calligraphy that Tosan inked to lame, inflame the gait, disable.*

*She remembers:
The danna's shoe, the symbols taking shape
returning pain for pain, for which the geisha paid
a hundred cakes. A hundred yen in purple money.*

The Girl They Hired From Snow Country

"Carry me," I said,

clutching at the hemp
too good to throw away—her rough kimono,
my sling my stink my blanket.

My father asks if I remember: The strong back,
my radar bouncing off the mountain of her shoulder,

how absence nursed me,

my mother happy to be rid of tadpoles, the others
flushed in buckets. My sister eating mud,
pulling out her hair, counting backwards.

She carried me all day until it rained so hard
the ghosts showed up.

"Carry me," they said.

Leaving the Emperor's Summer House

ironweed turning
rusting the pond—shadows
of wild geese, leaving

In Hirohito's house my father lives in the collapse of silk. He speaks the language. In a dolphin-gray kimono, he wears a moustache thin as Errol Flynn's, bows to options from Nigeria. Offshore rigs. The floating world of sake, yellow fin. A strange cocoon of bars on back streets of the Ginza's grid. Kabuki. Hot springs.

A photograph. My father with my mother in a winter mink, her bangs cut straight, her belly big.

Tea thins.

My father trades for passport. To pay the girl they hired from snow country, he trades the mink.

"We'll always have …," my mother would begin, like Ilsa. The scene from *Casablanca*. The fall of Tokyo like Paris.

In photographs they wear the drab-green coats she fashioned from surplus Army blankets.
The stove's a pit of ashes.

Bonsai

                      Space

                                      is open   silence
Roots trained
      in containment. The tray—

                                a flat clay stunned
                                              Defeat

that strips to leave the least
bare branch that bears
      the keloid of the cut
            Shears, benders, cutters

                                              Wind-implied
                                                 disaster

              How to make us small

                   These
                   trees

                   survive
                    dis-
                  figured

Two

First sounds of a small drum

The World As Seen Through Bottled Coke is Bigger, Mr. Moto

Houses made of paper disappear. Beneath the turbulence of clouds a checkerboard of farms in Pennsylvania. Ten thousand things release, a thousand born.

Original Child

> *I. The Originator—Tokyo to Guam, the United States*

Land and sky the same wing-gray.
The air, like atoms, heavy.

We board as we are born: The point of all departure.

Rounder-eyed. Bangs cut straight.
"Please," she says for paper cranes.
Her mouth a portal. A blossomed sayonara.

They bring her cookies on a plate.
They bring the milk her mother hates.
A pillow book of rain.

> *II. Learning losing—one two three*

Counting on her fingers: "ichi ni…."

"Shi"—means death or she who reads from wrong
to left, the alphabet's translation.
The Japanese "ohio" means good morning.

Out of turbulence like play
words she can't pronounce.

Ketchup. Fork. Surrender.

Translation

I sat in your lap, the words in mine

like "bear" in the book, like Pooh in a tightness of bees.
You gave me sweets,

as if sweetness could honey
the words between us, the worlds,
the syllables you struggled,

the language that you taught yourself
teaching me.

L's instead of r's, lice instead of rice.
"Sink," you said,
when you meant "think."

I mischiefed meaning,
tumbled easy into speech.
How to translate grief?

Unheard, how to repeat?

Your voice floated   disconnected,

like a bubble in a cartoon strip.
"Sink," you said. *Sink.*

Breakages in Japanese

"See?" Okaasan said, as if unwrapping fish.
"These are not the geta.
You can take big steps."

It rained all day
through cat-and-dog translations.
Bug, dug, fun. Gud, duf, nug.

Words like happy children skipped across my desk—
through forests great as Gretel's.

Sister Theresa Martin gave us cardboard letters.
She gave us milk Okaasan hates.

"Only boys wear brown," the girl in ribbons said,
laughing at the boots under my desk.

Ducking under elbows, into rooms with yellow pencils,
I had to take three steps for every one of theirs.

"Run run run!" said vowels from *Dick and Jane*.
The "u" an upside-down umbrella.

A Rose, Twice My Size

—For Tokyo Rose

>Why didn't she go home
before they found resemblance
in snapshots at Sugamo Prison?

>1946, the schoolgirl's smile—inscrutable
as FBI. Why

>haul me, arms and legs across a play-
ground buckeye bombed? Why

>swing me like a rope for fox-in-geese,
fling me into dislocation?

>Broken shoulder. Broken stem.

>They say she sang like crow on short-wave radio,
though broadcasts of her singing don't exist

>or scripts
turned up missing.

Two faces, one facing east,

*the other with its gaze in the direction of the tracks that ran the brilliant coal
to old Donora.*

*We crossed from oven gas and hammer, from furnaces to streets we named
by trial and error,
those nights played backwards, the sound system blasting,
the Ford souped up and sliding greased into the neon of the diner.*

*Heat-pocked tribes with blackened faces:
Zdunowski. Flanigan and Conte.
All of Africa in Smokey Robinson.*

*Dosed on opium from Thailand, licks of window pane,
we worked the graveyard shift like ants in fire. Hallucinated angels.
The center less and less familiar—the means to ends
in cryptographs occulted on the headphones,
revelations in the residue of Fanta cans*

before Angang. Wuhan. Tangshan,

*where mountain kneels to blossom,
where river ferries toads,*

*where plums are pickled
like carbon steels.*

No reason to go home before we're lost.

Earthquake Thunder Fire Father

Elbows and our knees served his inspection
against the hubris of cartoons, the laziness too soon
ingrained. He trained us kids in grunt campaigns
on Saturdays. No R&R. No sleeping in.
The tv room off-limits until mattresses were stripped,
brooms soldiered, a load of whites on spin.
We reconnoitered under dust-ruffles for socks/safety pins,
Hoovered every room, Ajaxed tub/sink,
bleached a booby trap of stink, worked the win-
dows up to specs, spit and shined until a finger left
no line on tables/dressers/desks. No surrender
to the dust drafted in like parachutes. No retreat.
It left him Patton-pleased if all was regulation.
To duty we saluted, to thunder and the dread.
"We should have gone into Korea"
is what he always said.

The Girl Who Loved Mothra

A mutant wing you know to be mechanical seems
real as faces in the front row lit by the projection.

Faces dimly seen until the screen explodes with the artillery.

A theater of war, where weapons don't prevail:
toy tanks, toy helicopters dropping nets.

U.S. lightening—useless in the fight against bad sequels.

I bunker in the radiated glow, bug eyed, caterpillar eyebrows
inching up over
glasses to inspect the giant wing, like the fan of the warrior

unfolding,
guarding unloved offspring.

O, monstrous egg.
O, prodigy
of wind and aberration
hatching twins.

Hide the Daughters, Hide the Rice

Scene 1
In sun and shadow sensei shoots the Western.
Sound of drum and weeping.

Is she worth the rice he pays? The price the farmer fears…
hungry ronin. Bandits riding, hooves on hardened earth.

The barley not yet in, the farmer fears the sun the rain the wind.

Okaasan with a baby on her hip serves ginger sliced like skin
in bowls with rice, she serves the cherry ice cream father likes.
Kirin beer in bottles, bowing to his lips.

I fetch the bowl, the beer, his slippers.
From rice I learn to simmer.

Scene 2
The son he never fathered in the person of a daughter
who hides where flowers court.

Okaasan ties my knees inside the folds of a kimono,
teaches me to hide inside a field of folding flowers.
Teaches me to hide the laughter lacking grace.

"You should have been a son," her father once had told her,
the soldiers riding in, horses on their shoulders.

I learn that beauty is a sack of running rice.

Scene 3
Losers cast as winners. Buddha as Yul Brynner.
Magnificent, the seven incarnations.

Paper in her hands becomes a frog, a crane.
A hat like the admiral's.

We play inside all day. Okaasan draws two figures
on a rainbow-bridge.
A man and a woman with a spear
or a stick.

Ten thousand things become, a thousand die in fire.

Wedding of the Foxes

If you happen as a child
on the wedding of the foxes,

the slow, strange procession
to the bridge of mist,
the bride's white approach
on flute and stealthy drum—

do not hide. Run
if vulgar scent gives you away,
if pines reveal what you are stealing
in the pockets of your eyes.

Never ask: Why this is that
or why sometimes the hand becomes
a paw, reaching into forests. Run

to where the sun bends into sudden colors,
where your mother waits behind the sliding screen
to see if it is you, knocking,

answers in her fox's voice disguised as "no" or "die,"
answers as she hands you
the dagger.

Silent Fish, Blushing Ginger

Where fish heads stir
suspicion,

where pickled ginger
pinks,
no clever integrations.

No plum sauce on a hot dog.
Tofu sliders.

My mother eats in silence
in the kitchen.

"HI, IN AMERICA"

you talk on cell phones
in the library…the ching chong ling long ting tong

blah blah blah…disrupting the epiphanies of others
A rising tide

against the wake. The hordes
buying groceries cooking food doing laundry
checking in

with whole! families lacking manners

children never fending for themselves, never independent
…disturbing

what we're sourcing from the Internet

oh, that skewered wig, those fishnet stockings
that dragon-lotus print for $19.99
For just one night

to play the "pink salon," the frottage
The cricket in the cage of some desire

Luckily, for crickets
a short life

What's up, honorable doc?

*All this talk talk talk
of kamikaze,
as if I'd bombed Pearl Harbor!*

*To belong, I sang along—
Perry Como, Tony Bennett. Frank Sinatra in his opera
from teen idol to Old Blue Eyes—so sure*

*he was American. Like Dinah Shore
who blew a kiss, as if she meant it,
as if she really wanted you to
"See the USA*
                    in your Chevrolet…."
I went along

*for the ride—stopping at the pool hall. The taxi stand.
Vinnie's Diner where the men cut creases in their pants
as sharp as knives as*

*Mr. Moto buys
the ice cream that explodes.*

Butterfly's Difficult Kata

By eight I knew the aria by heart. "Un bel di" reprised—me
singing Lucy singing Yoko singing Cio-Cio-san.

To make her laugh, I crawled across the floor to where
she steeped the tea to please.
I practiced death in scenes—

flip-flops for the geta on my feet, cotton bathrobe for kimono,
a butter knife for dagger. I staggered—

doubled over. She
doubled over—

laughing *(un bel di)*.

Moon in the Water

The barge is a mountain moving shadows
A long, slow coming

I see in waking
a rat-face fat as grandma's
laughing in debris

The belly in a beer can

The plastic bag that weeps

The driftwood to the tide
surrenders at the brink

The river lurks in babble
It waves against hard places

tugs at moonlight
signaling the ripple
I cuff my jeans

the waves reaching to the bone inside my knees
The moon throws out its buoy
The moon in water saves me

Three

The love and death of Izanami

Geisha

All day she had not cried.
Obaasan was pleased.

She showed her the drawer
in the cabinet—the drawer with its lacquered moon

                                        drifting—
                                                the drawer
inlaid with pearl, where she hid the fine chocolates.

It was winter and no one had chocolates.
It was winter and few had rice
             —the drawer
                    with its moon off center

like sweetness inside the dark.
She said, "This is what you get when you are very good."

Origami

                         A paper
      crane in   sequences
   of hexagons, rectangles   A blade of grass, wings
   of beetles   Anything in less than 30 steps   We fold
the calculations   What good a paper house   when bombers
fly so low she   sees the gunners' faces   What good a bamboo
  stick against a gun   The city   that was Tokyo in reflex
                    convex angles

Floating World

Aiko shoos the dragonflies that spark through green bamboo.
                    The nursemaid in the cuckoo's tattle, naps.

                  Viewed
             from all angles—
                   slant of roof,
             blush of sun—

anthurium inclines,
       upward from its shining leaf erect.

                         Maidenhair a pretty purple
               spreading.

She unties her sash.

Nothing in this floating world but happy impulse.
        Plum wine in the basket.

1947

While she waits for him to pilfer from the post exchange the little sandwiches of processed cheese, little packages like money up his sleeve, she plays Monopoly. Takes lessons in the English language. The others tease the one who stands her chopsticks in her rice. "Here comes grandpa for you."

Black markets getting blacker at the Red Cross canteen.

Tunnel

Ribs of soot. Dim
fluorescence.

She snaps,
"noisy, noisy"
at us huddled in the back
of the Chevy sunk
in shadow.

No radio.
No horseplay.
No sound
at the center.

Taillights
fill the sockets of her eyes.
A disembodied
hand
rolls up
the window,

honking
raids her back.
A dead friend's hand

rising
from the ashes.
Skin the same freak-
gray as poisoned rain,
as nameless flowers

until headlights merge with light, a river she remembers
as the sea. We drink our bellies full of tea
in a restaurant in an alley, where the girl who looks like us
serves up Fortune in the cookie no one wants.

The Hare—
                is me
              furred
reserved
One chopstick balanced like a pencil

the other like a wing against my finger
The table's set with zodiacs on placemats
Aiko is the cock (Beware
the opposite and greedy)
begging for the parasol that floats
in dangerous slings

The monkey is my brother begging "fries." "Real food"
not won ton soup, not noodles

Etsuko wags her chopstick
"No flies," she says
I slurp the noodles

Fortune's in the freeze
not in the cookie

Salmon Says Surrender

Perhaps she doesn't hear—"Jap"—
long after the surprise attack
the armless man, his sleeve pinned
back, perhaps a veteran of the word
surprises back—"Jap"—
at the fish market in Pittsburgh
her troubled accent asks, "Reeve head, preeze"
for meat in cheeks, in eyes (delicacies)
over the frenzied scaling—"Jap"—
the lust of capture in the brine
the buckets overrun with gutted monk
to wrap—"Sa-mon!"—she cries
The casualties of tuna begging on the ice
The incense left long after the beheading

My mother's in bare feet, squatting like a refugee, yesterday's Daily Republican *spread out bloodied on the kitchen floor in front of her. She's plucking feathers from a bird (pheasant? quail?) or flaying a riddled rabbit. We never know. Whatever it is, we'll find it in the sauce for dinner. If we ask, sometimes she tells the truth, sometimes she lies—especially if she thinks that we won't eat it. Aiko complains the sauce tastes "funny." I fork the grayish lump. "What is it?" "Chicken," she says, smiling, as if to remind us: All is illusion.*

My father says the Japanese are sneaky.

Rice

Father said you must be mindful. Never hurry. Wash it twice—
once to get the milky rinse and if the second wash runs clear,

press your hand into the pebbled surface of the grain
like starfish fingers in the sand.

Run water just to cover
like rock over paper, paper over rock,
like his hand over mine in the pot.

A monument of starfish over starfish in the sand.

I understand. This is how we boil without burning, rattle and
release in paste that shoulders rim.

The simmer seems a lifetime
at the sound of the bell.

At the sound of ourselves
becoming, how quickly we eat!

Translation

Sound is an image—the instrument of rain becoming rain:

                     The pichi-
                        pichi
choppu-choppu   rain.

How to say in syllables of water?
My mouth is a child asking names.

Oishii is delicious, yes? A bowl of miso soup.
Long rice, noodles.

Okaasan is a mother's tongue
running with umbrellas.

Chopsticks

What sustains you is
beyond their lacquered reach.

Twin bridges.
The forced beak
of your fingers is
the bird you want to be,
pecking at the bowl of it,
the empty dish.

If on the plate the salmon's head
points to the door,
does that mean
you always will be
leaving?

The places you enter are never the same:
The places you set at the table.

The body guides
its appetites
as wings clear
the gate.

You can take
only so much
between the tips.

A pinch of grain, a sliver.

Dream-Box Essay

When the Emperor surrendered, everyone surrendered.
Everyone in tears except the Chinese opera singer.
A knife in the sleeve of Nanking.

Something's falling with the snow.

A house of flesh- and crayon-colored brick.
Not optical effect

but memory of a "house" when I think "house."
As when light strikes
its opposite,

something's caught.

Straw and sticks turned upside down.
Four walls squaring off,
rooms with least exposure.

A camera obscura.

A photograph: My father as a metaphor of absence.
My mother in mute presence…cornered like an animal.

Forty-Eight Positions

Fallen Cherry Blossoms
First of Summer in the Resin Pine

Under lyrical titles
how they came to flesh in colors!

Cudgel and thief. The insatiable bonze.
The lord with tongue and fingers.

A sumptuous unfolding
I took for quarrel.

A scroll with brush strokes of kimonos

flung open.

Red Japonica

No matter that the silk forgives the worm,
the table on its legs forgives the weight.

No one to forgive the daughter who betrays
a family's name, a brother's honor.
No one on her side. They never write,

her house in Florida in exile, pretending
plums for the occasion.

Dolls with painted faces, painted vases, painted screens.
Panels of the seasons. The iris and chrysanthemum.

And to the east,
outside the sun room,
culms of grooved bamboo in bone meal, urns
of red Japonica, cascading.

SHE WHO LISTENS TO PUCCINI

Even though her tongue never bowed
to his articulations
he made her in the way
Pygmalion created
she who was milkwhite—
Galatea

Tokyo the ivory from which he carved Eliza

He named her as a variant of Mary
A cultivated pearl
Jade to furnish graves
Even though he married
"Maria" to the states
she remained

She Who Drinks Green Tea
She Who Listens To Puccini

Even now he wonders if she loved him

Katana

Sometimes my father adds a detail, another "fact" in the narrative of Occupation. Etsuko laughs at his version of her liberation from roving bands of ronin at Tokyo's railway station. But he insists: The scar is true as any wound. The surgeon's cut with scalpel resembling slash of steel. The smile below the navel a wink at truth. I want to hear again how he saved her. I want to grieve. Not for the lies he tells but for the sword he keeps as souvenir. The great katana: Soul of the samurai—hammered, forged. Like facts we can't remember, truths we can't ignore. There was love. There was war. It cut both ways.

Seven Enemies

"Not a bad word about him."

One might interpret this as people offered cakes,
he healed their ailments,

but when Obaasan sniffs, as if there were a stink,
Etsuko says that what she really means is
he'd left them only

broken statues, broken carvings,
facades from ruined temples—
restoration his obsession.

Like the sword he polished in the dark
after Hirohito had surrendered.

She means: A man who is
               a man

strides out of his house each day
to face seven enemies.

Four

Snow

Memorial Day Parade, 1957. Ticker tape sticks to her bangs, to the sleeves of her pink kimono, to the small hand that props the American flag—on the boulevard named for the dead.

Autobiographia Hysteria

The dark self like ink
like Hiroshige's views—rain
in Edo. Mountain!

Nothing of my mother's flower lips.

Nothing to explain the suffering of my look.
The manners of exclusion…"you are overly sensitive,
they said…you are…?"

I stood at the bridge
between dogs of earth
and the sun who is my true father.

Between enemy and friend.
Ambiguities a dark kimono.

I might have been a thief, scrounging in the prefectures.
The outcast "freak." China doll, a whore.
A fetish from the war that never ends.

I could kill them with my countries of forgiveness.
I could kill them with the smallness of my hands.

Reconciliation—that dagger.

Teenage Ninja-Geisha

In scarves & costume jewelry the crew-cut cop who cuffs me
yanks—my heavy lids translated

"Frankly, dear, I'm quite surprised to see your kind
shoplifting here"

Caught red-handed with the loot
Never sorry, never cute
Never coy like Ah-So's serving rice & soy
Like Butterfly who'd rather die
than lose a little face—not

this red-blooded Jap
This dotheadflatheadslitslope
Nope

No cheap transistors in my head
No seppuku for a stolen cardigan
Think again

I like Ike I like Spam I like American Bandstand

I'm the gook with U.S. papers
The geek with hyphenation
The Yellow Peril realized
in teenage ninja-geishas

Iris and the Blade

—*For Mishima*

The body Japanese

perfect as the death
you posed for, exposed

to arrows. A saint
A temple burning, crematory

like paper lanterns set adrift on mirrored seas

The sound of waves
perfect as the words—arranged

and you and you, seconded
The man the masks

the incarnations
inside out to show the cut

Rough flower of the spleen
The bright kimono, opened

The iris with its blade turned out

The incense of your death sweetens
skull, dulls

the longing for a country

Manzanar

Summer

The wind blows dust like hulls of rice.
They stand in line for everything.
Old or orphan doesn't matter. Not strong enough.

All of them fenced in like chickens.
"Keep busy. Do not think about the things that cannot change."

Winter

They used the lids from ration tins to cover holes in floors.
Nothing to the east but mountains rising up.
A white wall. Barbed wire.

Present

"Remember? It was all over sugar.
They thought he had a gun but it was only a light
bulb shattering."

It's no use fighting. What is life but dying?

Past

The buses came.
The signs in shops, nailed to fences: "Aliens and non-aliens
of Japanese ancestry report as ordered...."

One mother wore her hat and Sunday gloves to board the bus.
A few hanged themselves.
Only take what you can carry, they said.

Night

The moon is rising over Pleasure Park.
There is the waterfall, there is the pond
they dug with their hands.
See how the moon reflects?
In every sorrow there is joy.

Day

They dig and carry stone, plant trees, write their poems under water, on supports.
On the concrete settling basin: "jap camp."

Leaves in the pear tree shiver.
Who is grieving for this floating world?

Ghost

Every night you cry into your sleeve.
I hear you call my name.

The things that used to make me happy only hurt me now.
The sun rising over mountains breaks my heart.

Bird

Again and again, I crash into glass.

My father, my mother:
my country.

I was born but have no place to rest.

To Stand in the Spaces of Trees

"Push," my father said, though he was only in my head.
"Push with your fists"—tamping ground,
packing it with shoulder set
to relocation. Watering to drench,
to compensate for debt
of soil.

I put my back into it,
roots drilled down,
balled tighter
than expected,

a fob of compact
dirt and worms,
the tiniest of spiders.

FIVE

puka puka—
sound
rain on slanted ocher clay
roof shoes muddied, small

Pictures in Bufano's Garden

—For the Hibakusha

Stick men in explosion. A young man's face, red with burns and
ruined, the glass and wood embedded.

Another face to show the ones who did not make it:
Four eyes, two noses, two mouths.

Pictures that a child might draw to tell what he remembers—
the barracks hit, the wind and blood hotter than the sun—but

cannot say in English to the small group gathered
in Bufano's sculpted garden.
A halting word-for-word translates:
Left in trenches
with the dead. A crematorium.

With tripod and a timer, he takes the picture.
A moment he translates: eyes, noses, mouths.
Another picture for himself, with himself in it.

Fukushima

>Teach us how to suffer
>ruined rice.
>Paddies in debris.
>
>The note on the wall
>plainly reads:
>"Fusiko, where are you?"
>
>Most of the plume
>blows out to sea.

Epicanthic Fold

unyielding cold, glacial adaptation old

as ice. Aboriginal,

                       the turgid lid
the swollen seeing/looking in
self-conscious-

ness   drift-of-self-
               esteem

swallows laughter in the slit, that eye…puff throated, folding
into nothingness adapted to the snow of flesh in treason

homogenous eye
homogenous spies: Observe

the smiling "yes" for "no"   the bowing low—
inscrutable

hooded, adder eyed, impossible to hide—surrender

Japanesque

New green shoots.
The channels pearled
like gifts to farmers
who have girls. Fields
becoming wetlands.

They plant, plant again.

More mood than color, more habit of the fishing boats
in Hokusai's moon, toward which she is impressioned.
A cartoon face—white against kimono's russet-red and gold,
the many greens that seem a forest,
the many patterns of the iris—
gazing toward the shamisen that represents
her talent for accompaniment.
The little cartoon mouth the art of silence.
A fan to practice shyness.
A hat, as if going,
though nowhere is she going
in that snow,
in those geta as ephemera.

SELF-PORTRAIT

Find me a color that fits like skin.

Language, belief, something to eat
that doesn't stare back
like fish in a bamboo steamer.

In the dream of a white girl
my tongue was one of theirs.

In the dream of a white girl
I was color

of poppies. Yellow
when they wanted

tattoo of chrysanthemum. Skin
of the bomb.

Iwo Jima. Flanders fields.
What did I know about crosses?

Furin

After years of no-wind talking,
I wouldn't bend,

                        unlike my sister, pretty as defense,
                        unlike my brother, always better
                        than the self he showed himself.

How memory works forward—I sent the chimes the day she
bought them for herself. The tenor
of a likeness. A mutual arising.
A thousand miles away, a single impulse.

"You must learn to be bamboo," she once had said.

O-Furo

I loved the pearls of soap that floated iridescent—I loved
when she scrubbed, the horned shampoo releasing suds
like clouds releasing demons.

My mother steeped in me like tea belief in nature's wisdom.
No sin to see her fallen breasts, the dark nipple that expressed
the nature that exhausted them.
The scar where I was called into the world.

Nakedness, not shame. Not weakness.

The legs
in legs, nesting
one
inside the other.

How could they know?
The ginkgo gives up dust when it rains—doesn't it?

How to Wear a Kimono

The weave before the war unfolds
in leaves in light repeating

The red azaleas haven't faded
Petals lifted blooming after years
from heavy-lidded cedar

The gold-brushed seam
of mountains glimpsed

The vein and bud as
she to me as
clan to mother

The measure of erotic in the collar

The sleeves as wings released
as if from their cocoon

How to shoulder
How to wear the tying over
sash and string

Hands like knives
through armholes under sleeves
to level silk

How to walk its length
The weight in little steps

How to dress occasions of
surrender   Wait
the sun's redress

How to guess the why   The way
we hate the things we hate

Before the war
Okaasan might have worn it
to a festival   Moon-gazing

THE WAY OF TEA

Coarse or finer substance matters.

Attend to how the thistle and camellia
picked that morning stand arranged,
how early evening wind ruffles the scroll,
how light infuses sorrow.

Put the kettle on to sigh.
Sprinkle water at the gate to let him know you are ready.
Let him leave his sandals at the door.

Bow, and when the door is softly closed
level powder, scoop the water to the bowl
with your finger at the joint.

Name the ladle cup of moon.
Name the mouth the taking.

Distinguish every sweetness.
Say, this is the only sweetness.

Six

Epilogue

She Who Invites

Izanami stands on a wooden bridge, her long black hair in a knot. Her red kimono dances with the pattern of the carp. She dips a bamboo spear into the mirror of the water and the universe begins. Dragonflies and skimmers. Fishes into frogs into birds on slender wings. A fox steps out, leaving paw-prints in the path that foxes take. A wolf. Six white horses. A family of monkeys. Izanami stirs the waters of the world.

Sirens near—her hair
in flames, her lashes—

Ten thousand things release, a thousand born...these are all distinctions.

Like the language of their hands, the garlic of a faith that had sustained them against the Evil Eye. Mussolini. The jewelry of rosaries.

They made their presence in the States the necessary freight of every mill, every railroad.

*The old man asks
what might be my interest in this place*

*my mother hates,
this place.*

*"O sole mio. Sta 'nfronte a te!"
—a likeness in the longing: Another sun. Another country.*

"Old Country."

Festival of Season Words

I was born in the moon of the seventh month. The waters clear, receding—no longer muddied by the small deer feeding, the sparrows circling rice fields or the snipe, shrike, wagtail quail migrating. In autumn's dry-voice leaves, the cicada cried "priest," the worms, small "ji." I was born in the literary moon. New coolness in a river of intensity. I feasted on the clouds of mackerel (*refreshing*), listened for the leaf-drop "pow" of the pawlonia, sound of scarecrow fulling blocks. The first storm opening to dusk. I was born in the moon of the seventh month.

The Japanese Have Stopped Having Babies

Hey, Joe. That top hat never passes "Go."
Never lands the deed for Park Place.
You patron undesirables,
the freetered refugees in net cafes
from Canada, the Philippines,
to the Caribbean. A hellish board
game of *karoshi*. (They said)
you cured the nun of her distemper,
after which, the girdle was a miracle
only Mark and Luke had bothered to
commit to gospel. (They said) your job
was load beam, fathering the contradiction.
Your staff promoting lilies lush but limp.
Odd tekton: Work. Eat. Work. Sleep.... Work.

Little Zeros

Such clatter at the gate!

They stagger up from bloodied knees,
the ginkgo in defeat. First surrender
in the cherries. The colors of the season
in explosion.

They fist and strike, zero in, nose diving,
swipe at banners of the leaves,
the asters in the western fire, dying.

One older, looks like me. The other passes
in his features for what's white—
seeds like peas in Mendel's garden
blown with winds

that war with trees. Seeds that can't be
summoned. The way of warriors
in their genes

"In self, those who are alive and dead"
—from the *Chandogya Upanishad*

A cane thumps. What does she want? Pointing to her lips. Should I offer?
The sun purpling hot. The bus about to stop

near the Medicine Shop. A daughter to her back—that furious hump?
She shoves a crumpled dollar for the trouble
that she is or she is not. A daughter without saying? To take the place
of one who's not?

Nanking is my mother.

Sayonaras

67 cities. A daughter in each

They walked to the outskirts. Everything they owned
in jellied gasoline, in sleeves of singed kimonos

In gray gardens of the napalmed streets
a small hand reaching

as if planted in the ashes. She was 17
"There was fire everywhere"
Etsuko says. "They were closing in"

The aerial view like Hartford
the size of Hamamatsu
Waves of gale-force winds

so hot. Self-sustaining in the drops
over Tokyo

Osaka/Kobe/Imabari
He died bravely
they said, the details

unavailable. A son
sent back as sand
A box

of dreams. "I saw him swimming
in the flames"
a mother says
Yokohama/ Kawasaki /Nagoya

The oil tankers
burning. The snow-
white mufflers all the same

Nagasaki/Hiroshima

Notes

Prologue. In 1926, a Japanese man from Boston named Shima Kito underwent cosmetic surgery to remove the slant in his eyes, because he wanted to marry his white girlfriend. Nineteen-hundred twenty-seven was year 2 of the Showa era, from December 25, 1926 to January 7, 1989. Showa ("Enlightened Peace") was the name of Hirohito's reign.

"Atonement." Taken from Emperor Hirohito's radio broadcast, accepting the Potsdam Declaration, August 14, 1945.

"Mr. Is-That-So?" Hirohito was nicknamed "Mr. Is-that-so?" by his Japanese subjects, because of his comments on visits to factories and schools after the war and during the Occupation. According to an October 1975 article in *The Japan Times* titled "Emperor Hirohito notified about Hiroshima A-bomb half day after," the Emperor when asked what he thought about the bombing told a news conference, "I feel sorry for Hiroshima citizens, but it couldn't be averted."

"Occupation." The period between 1945 and 1952, when U.S. occupying forces, led by General Douglas A. MacArthur, enacted widespread military, political, economic, and social reforms in Japan.

"Breakages in Japanese." The title is taken from a line in Gertrude Stein's *Tender Buttons*, in "Objects," under "Glazed Glitter": "There can be breakages in Japanese."

"A Rose, Twice My Size." For Iva Toguri, the most famous name linked to the "Tokyo Rose" persona. Though evidence showed she was not a Japanese sympathizer, Toguri's radio program became conflated with the propaganda, and she was arrested and convicted of treason after Japan's surrender. Togura, a native of Los Angeles, was released from prison in 1956. More than 20 years later, she received a presidential pardon.

"Earthquake Thunder Fire Father." From a Japanese saying which ranks the fearful things in order.

"The Girl Who Loved Mothra." Mothra is the "strange beast" monster that first appeared in Toho's 1961 film *Mothra*.

"Hide the Daughters, Hide the Rice." After Kurosawa's *Seven Samurai*.

"Wedding of the Foxes." After Kurosawa's *Dreams*. The Kitsune no Yomeiri, "the fox's wedding," commonly referred to as a sun-shower is an event told about in classical Japanese legends. It is the strange wedding procession that can be seen in light of unknown origin.

"Butterfly's Difficult Kata." After Puccini's opera *Madama Butterfly*, and after the 1962 American film *My Geisha*, in which a Hollywood actress disguises herself as a geisha. Kata are choreographed patterns of movements used in many traditional Japanese arts, in theatre forms like kabuki and schools of the tea ceremony, but most commonly known in martial arts. "Un bel di" ("One beautiful day") is the opera's most famous aria.

"Hi, in America." The quote is taken from the YouTube video "Asians in the Library," in which the former UCLA student Alexandra Wallace in the wake of the tsunami at Fukushima

Daiichi mocks the speech of Asian students and faults them for calling their families.

"Forty-eight Positions." Sexual positions inspired by the 48 basic sumo techniques. A bonze is a priest or monk.

"Red Japonica." After The Weeping Blossom Festival in late February.

"Katana." The traditional sword with a curved blade worn with the edge upwards in the sash; it was developed from the sword of the samurai class in the Edo period (1600s to late 19th century).

"Iris and the Blade." When unarmored, samurai would carry their sword with the blade facing up or "turned out." This made it possible to draw and strike in one quick motion.

"Manzanar." Located in California, Manzanar was the site of one of ten camps where over 110,000 Japanese-Americans were incarcerated during World War II.

"Pictures in Bufano's Garden." For Saito Masakazu, Nobuo Miyake, Takeharu Terao, survivors of the bombings of Hiroshima and Nagasaki. The Bufano Sculpture Garden is located at Johns Hopkins University in Baltimore, Maryland. Shortly after the United States entered World War I in 1917, the sculptor Beniamino Bufano accidentally cut off half of his right index finger and mailed it to President Woodrow Wilson as a protest against the war.

"Fukushima." After the earthquake and tsunami that triggered the nuclear accident on March 11, 2011 at Fukushima Daiichi and Hokusai's "Under the Wave off Kanagawa."

"How To Wear a Kimono." Moon-gazing. According to custom, the Japanese observe the new crescent moon, the moon on its

16th and 17th nights, and single out the full moon Chushu no meigetsu (mid-autumn moon) in the eighth month of the lunar calendar for particular admiration.

"THE WAY OF TEA." The Japanese tea ceremony.

"EPILOGUE." In Japanese Shinto-mythology, Izanami ("the female who invites") is a primordial goddess and personification of the Earth and darkness. She is the wife and sister of Izanagi, and together they created Onogoro, the first island of the Japanese archipelago. After Izanami died giving birth to the fire god Kagutsuchi, Izanagi went to the underworld to take her back with him but she refused, sealing the entrance to imprison him and vowing to kill one thousand of Izanagi's subjects a day, while Izanagi vowed to create fifteen-hundred new ones a day.

"LITTLE ZEROES." The "Zero" is a long-range fighter aircraft operated by the Imperial Japanese Navy from 1940 to 1945, referred to by its pilots as the "Reisen" (zero fighter), "0" being the last digit of the Imperial Year 2600 (1940) when it entered service. The Nanking Massacre, also known as the Rape of Nanking, occurred during the Second Sino-Japanese War when Japanese troops looted, raped and murdered the residents of Nanjing (then spelled Nanking), then capital of the Republic of China. The massacre occurred over six weeks starting on December 13, 1937. An estimated 50,000–300,000 died.

"SAYONARAS." In the 2003 documentary *The Fog of War: Eleven Lessons from the Life of Robert S. McNamara*, McNamara, the former U.S. Secretary of Defense, said that before the dropping of atomic bombs on Hiroshima and Nagasaki in 1945, under the command of General Curtis LeMay, B-29 planes firebombed 67 Japanese cities.

Acknowledgments

Grateful acknowledgment is made to the following publications, in which these poems, sometimes in earlier versions, first appeared: *The Apalachee Review, Asia Literary Review, Barnwood Poetry Magazine, Blue Collar Review, Bluestone Review, Bryant Literary Review, Cider Press Review, Clockhouse, The Doctor T.J. Eckleburg Review, Earth's Daughters, 88: A Journal of Contemporary American Poetry, Frogpond, Ginosko Literary Journal, Hawai'i Review, The Inflectionist Review, Japanophile, Juked, Kartika Review, Lantern Review, Mascara Literary Review, Memoir, Mythium, Natural Bridge, Now Culture, Pirene's Fountain, Platte Valley Review, Poecology, Poetry International, Prairie Schooner, Prime Number, The Sewanee Review, Silk Road, Southern California Review, Southern Poetry Review, Sycamore Review, Two Review, Waxwing, Witness,* and *you are here: the journal of creative geography;* and to these anthologies: *Manticore: Hybrid Writing from Hybrid Identities* (Sundress Publications); *Never Enough Flowers: The Poetry of Peace II* (The Nuclear Age Peace Foundation); *Nuclear Impact: Broken Atoms in Our Hands* (Shabda Press); and *Sunrise from Blue Thunder* (Pirene's Fountain).

Special thanks to Leah Maines at Finishing Line Press for publishing the chapbook *The Girl Who Loved Mothra,* in which some of these poems appeared; to the Maryland State Arts Council and the Baltimore Office of Promotion & the Arts for their generous support.

To Judy Cooper and the Enoch Pratt Free Library for hosting the first reading of these poems at Writers LIVE; to Aaron Henkin at WYPR for featuring my poems on the weekly podcast "The Signal"; to Judith Kerman at the Woodstock Mayapple Writers' Retreat for affording time and space for revision and Helen Ruggieri and Wendy Taylor Carlisle for the first manuscript critique.

To Barbara Diehl and Lalita Noronha, who have believed in me and provided generous feedback on some of the earliest versions of these poems.

I am indebted to the 'ohana at Saddle Road Press, and especially to Ruth Thompson for her beautiful vision and commitment to the lyric hybrid, and to Don Mitchell, for his expertise, his integrity of design, and his seemingly infinite patience.

About the Author

Half Japanese, Kathleen Hellen was born in Tokyo in 1951, six years to the day after Japan's surrender to the Allies. Her father served as secretary to the U.S. Defense Counsel for Prime Minister Hideki Tōjō during the Tokyo War Crimes Trials. Her mother was born into the military nobility of the samurai and the daughter of a Shinto priest.

Hellen is the author of the award-winning *Umberto's Night* and two chapbooks, *The Girl Who Loved Mothra* and *Pentimento*. Nominated for the Pushcart and Best of the Net, and featured on Poetry Daily, her poems have been awarded the Thomas Merton poetry prize and other prizes.

www.ingramcontent.com/pod-product-compliance
Lightning Source LLC
Chambersburg PA
CBHW030454010526
44118CB00011B/939